MW00873850

Hi, welcome to the fun way to learn about vehicles through 100 creative coloring pages!

Ideally suited for kids ages 1-4 as they discover the world around them. This book is intended to boost early childhood development through engaging activities that build connections with words, pictures and colors. All the custom artwork has been created by experienced designers to be the right level for kids to stimulate imagination, to allow them to build their fine motor skills and to have a load of fun and learning in the process!

With 100 big pages of illustrations, children will explore and enjoy a HUGE variety of easy to color vehicles.

Thank you for purchasing this book and we hope you and your little ones unlock a world of coloring fun and learning! We're still learning and growing ourselves, so we'd really appreciate a review on Amazon for this book if you have time. **Thank you.**

Check out other titles in our TODDLER COLORING series!

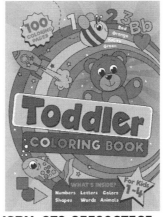

ISBN: 979-8552067565   ISBN: 979-8509492808

SUBMARINE

SPACE SHUTTLE

FORKLIFT TRUCK

DUMP TRUCK

CONCRETE MIXER

TRICYCLE

SPACE
CAPSULE

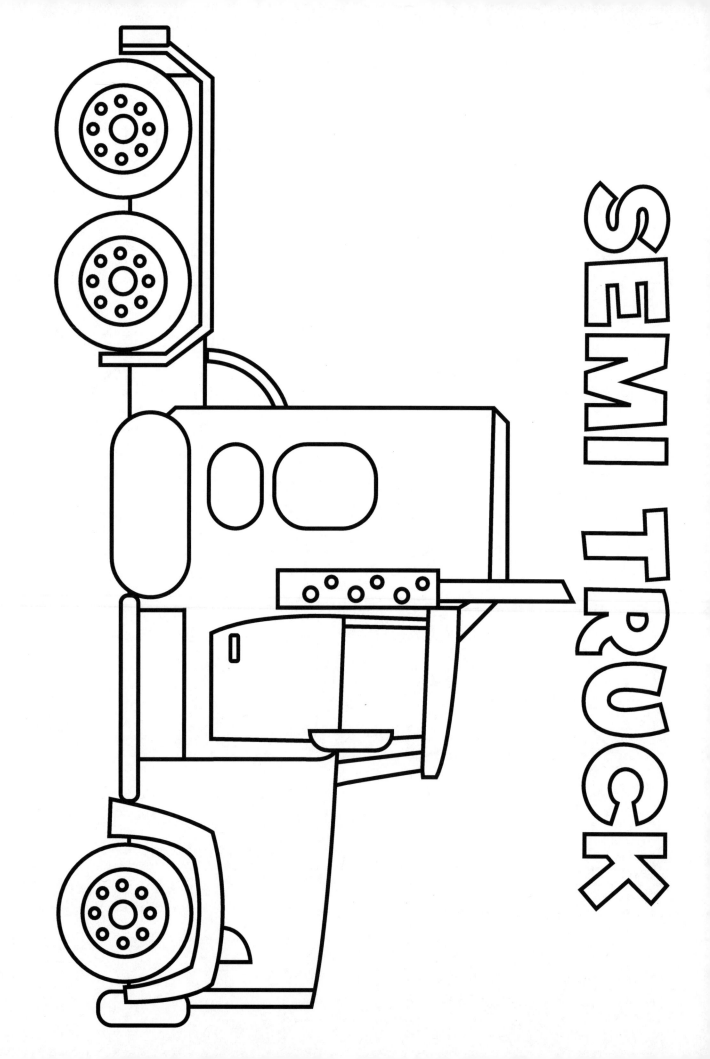

SEMI TRUCK

SCOOTER

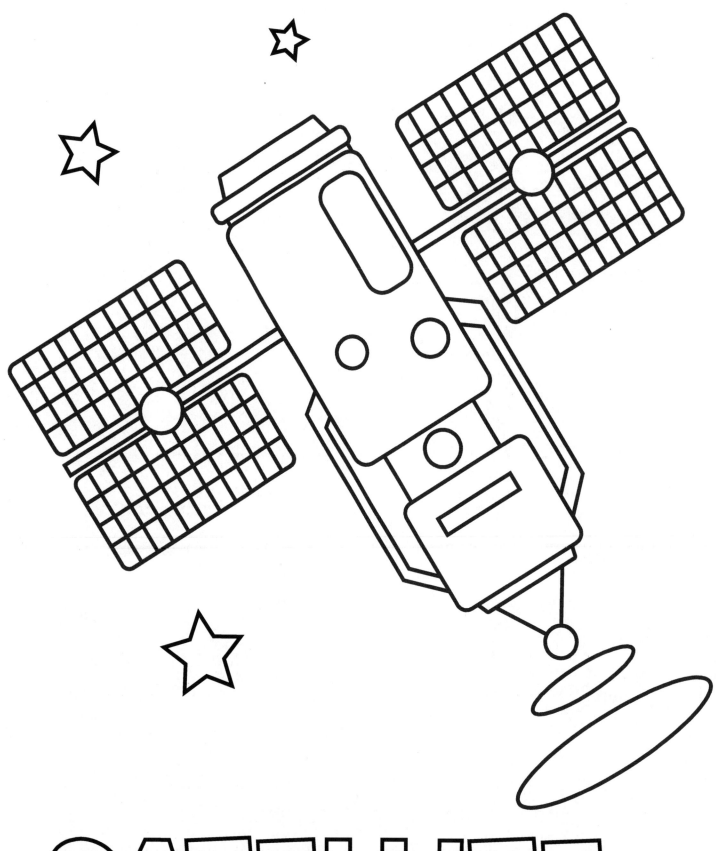

SATELLITE

TANKER

RICKSHAW

MOBILE CRANE

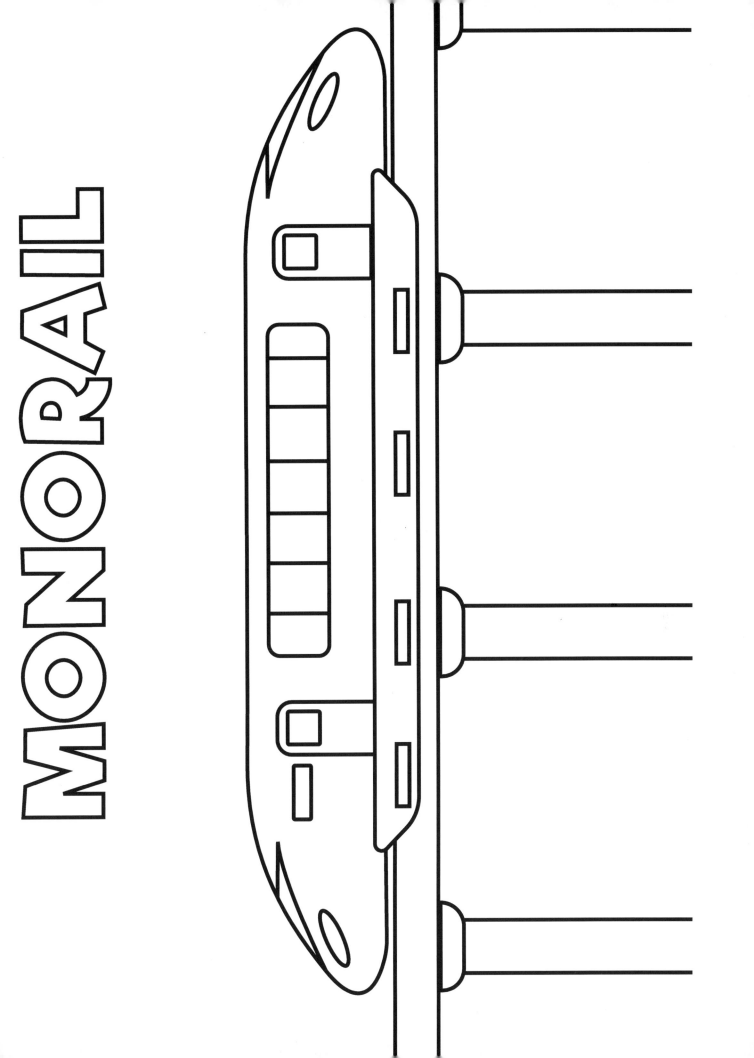

MONORAIL

KAYAK

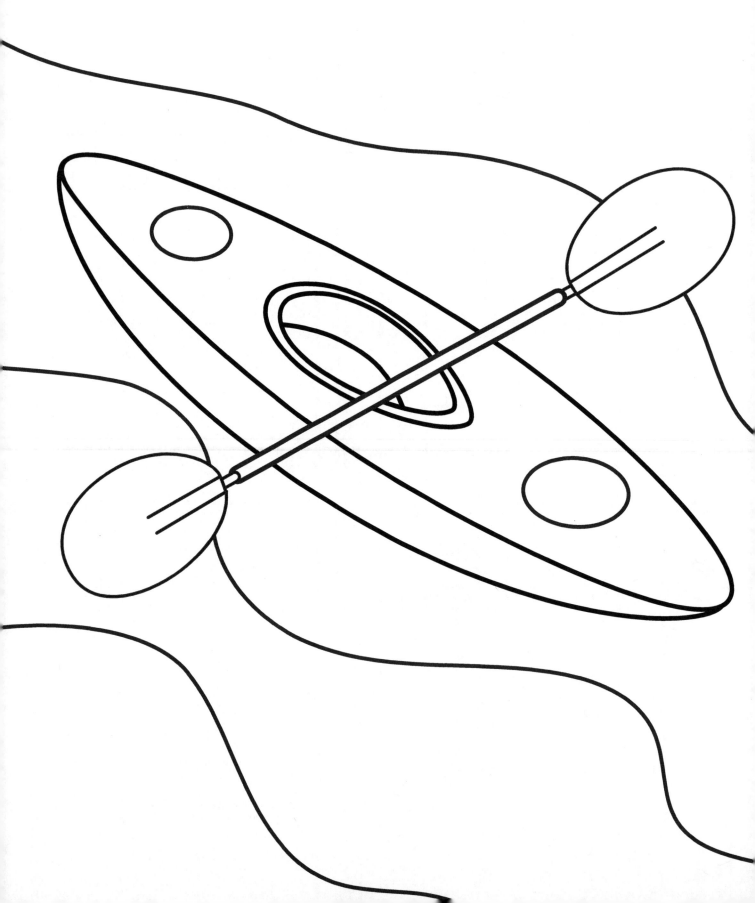

TOWER CRANE

POLICE MOTORBIKE

STAIR TRUCK

ICE CREAM TRUCK

FIRE TRUCK

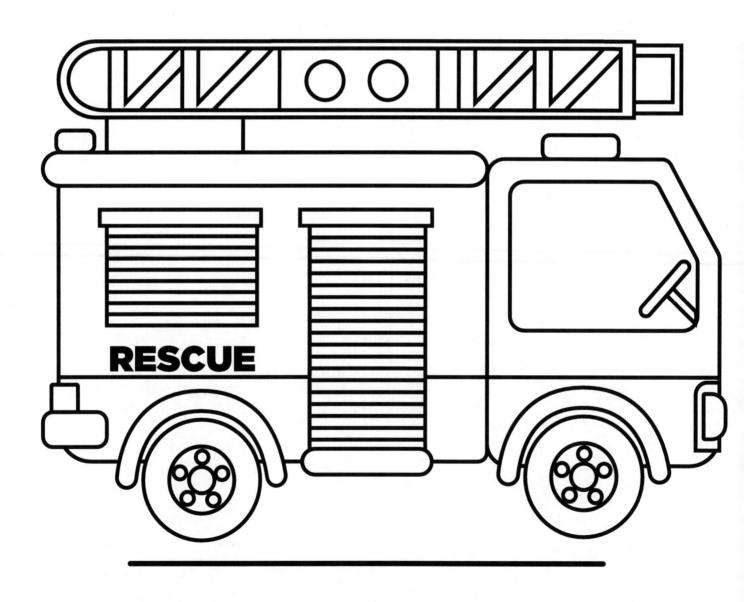

RESCUE

EXCAVATOR

AMPHIBIOUS VEHICLE

4x4
OFFROADER

HOT AIR
BALLOON

GOLF BUGGY

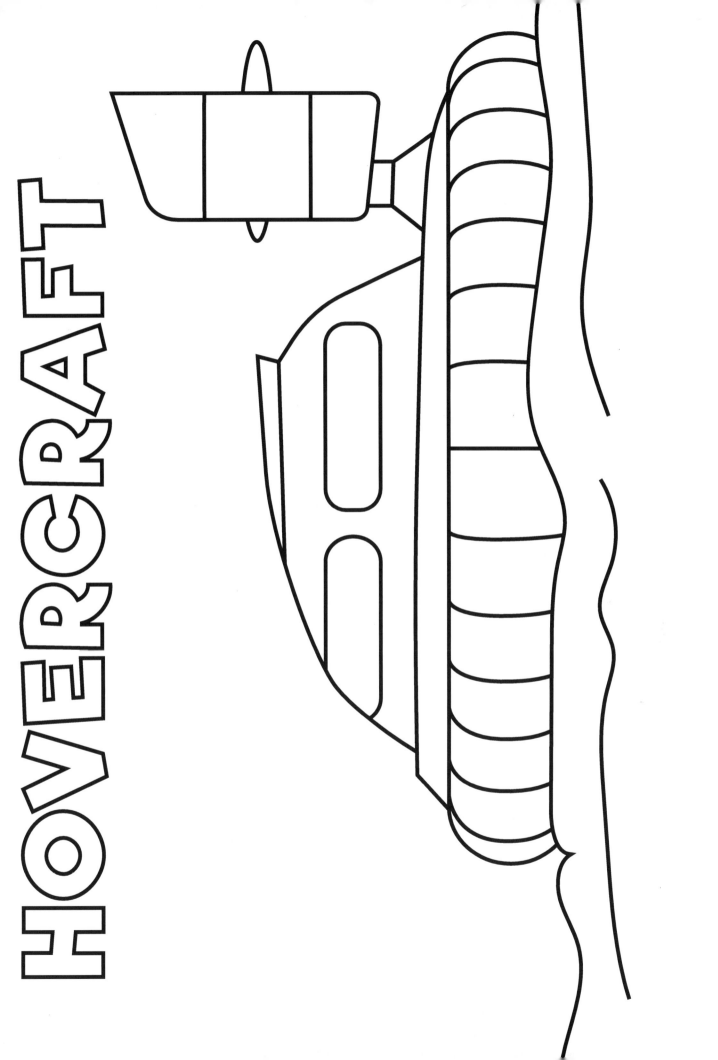

HOVERCRAFT

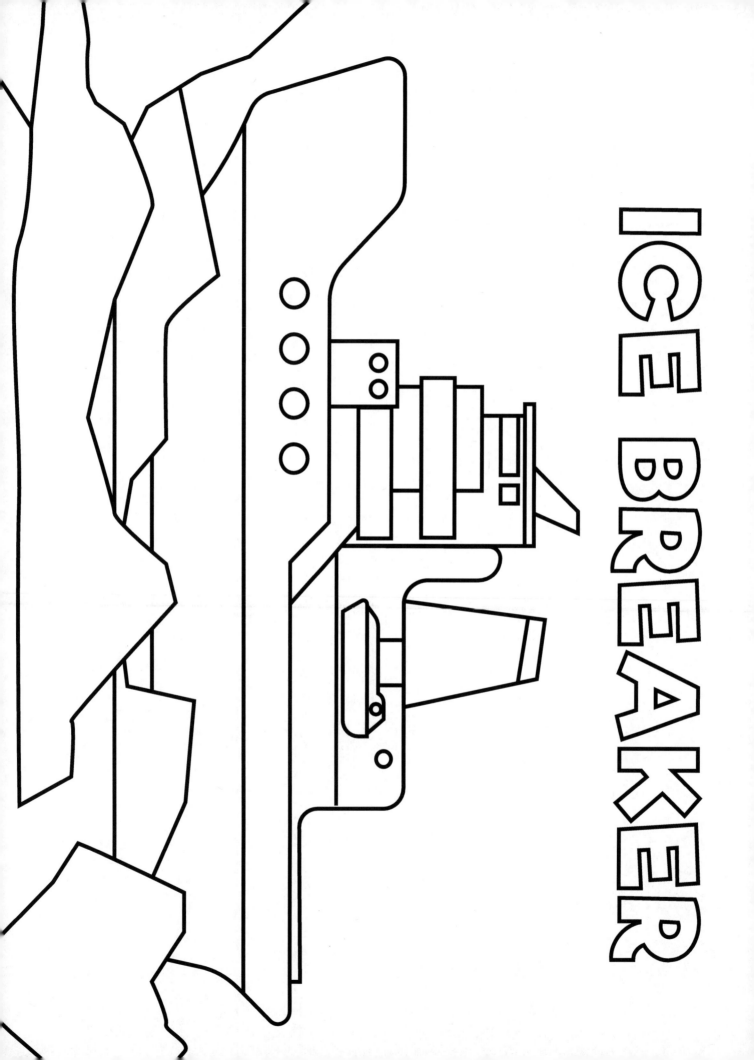

ICE BREAKER

ULTRALIGHT

WINDSURF

ROLLER COASTER

SNOWPLOUGH

MONSTER TRUCK

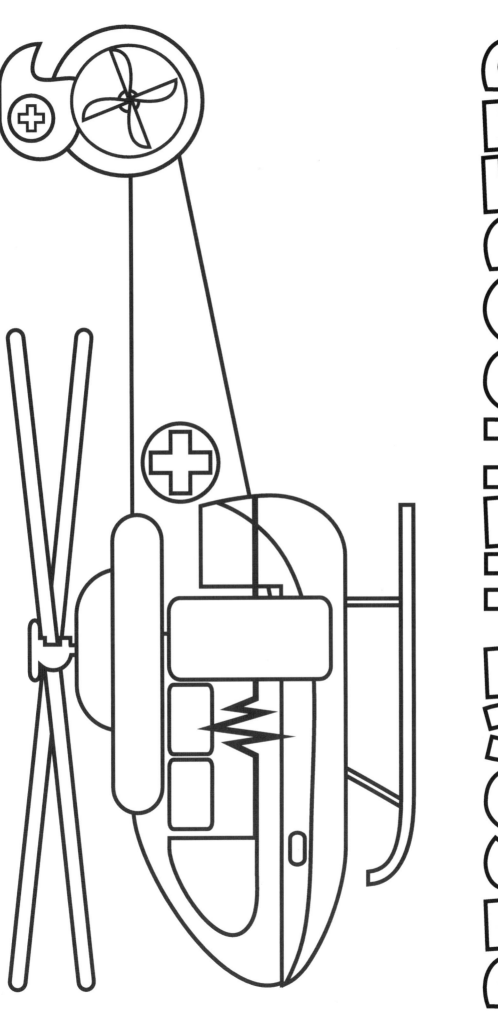

RESCUE HELICOPTER

LADDER FIRE TRUCK

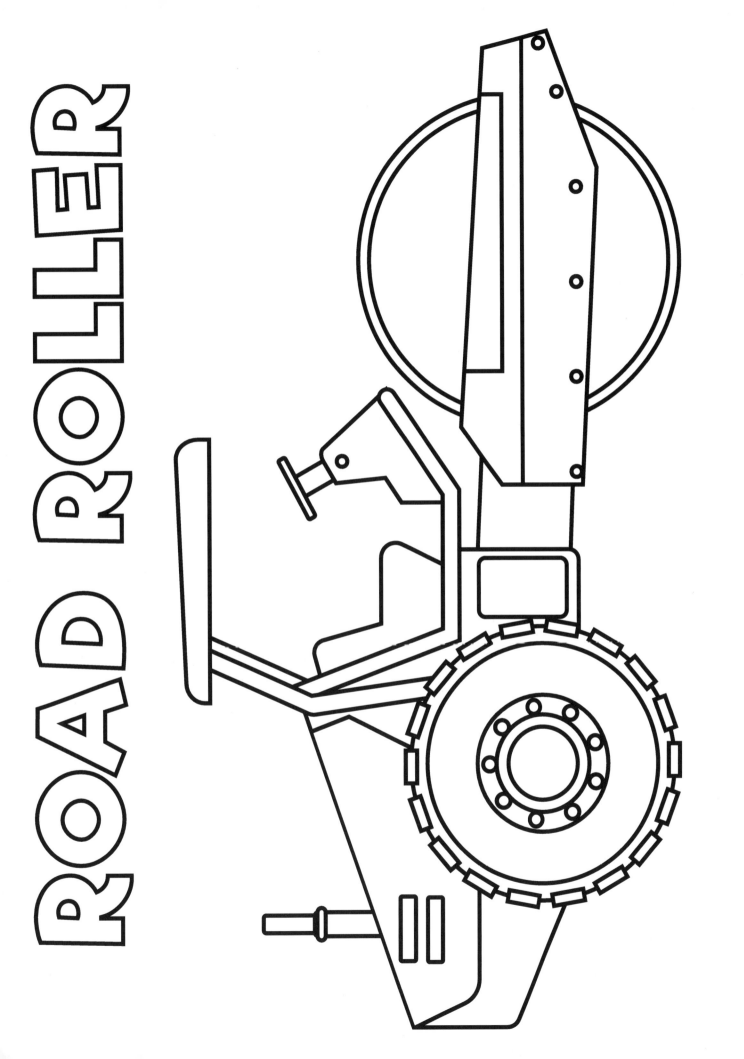

ROAD ROLLER

GARBAGE TRUCK

FISHING BOAT

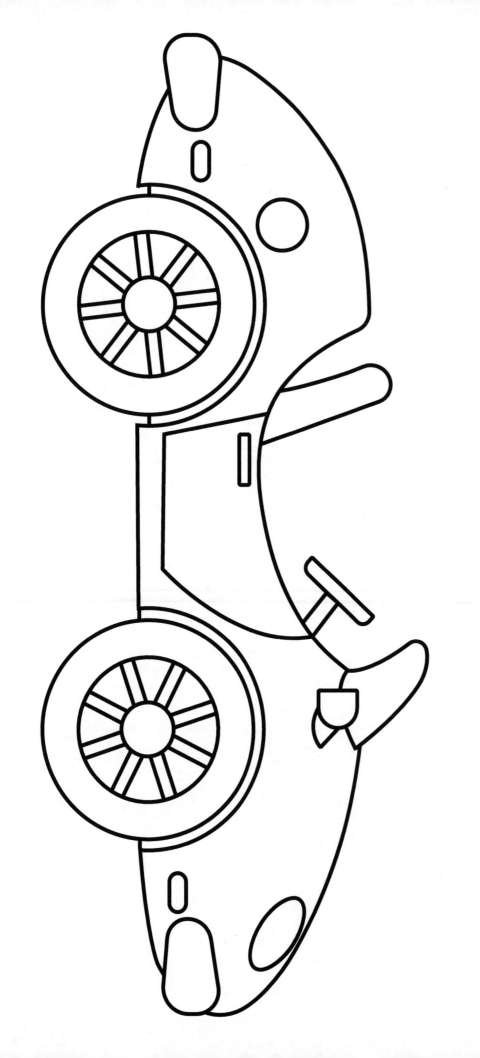

CONVERTIBLE

BULLDOZER

AIRPORT CATERING TRUCK

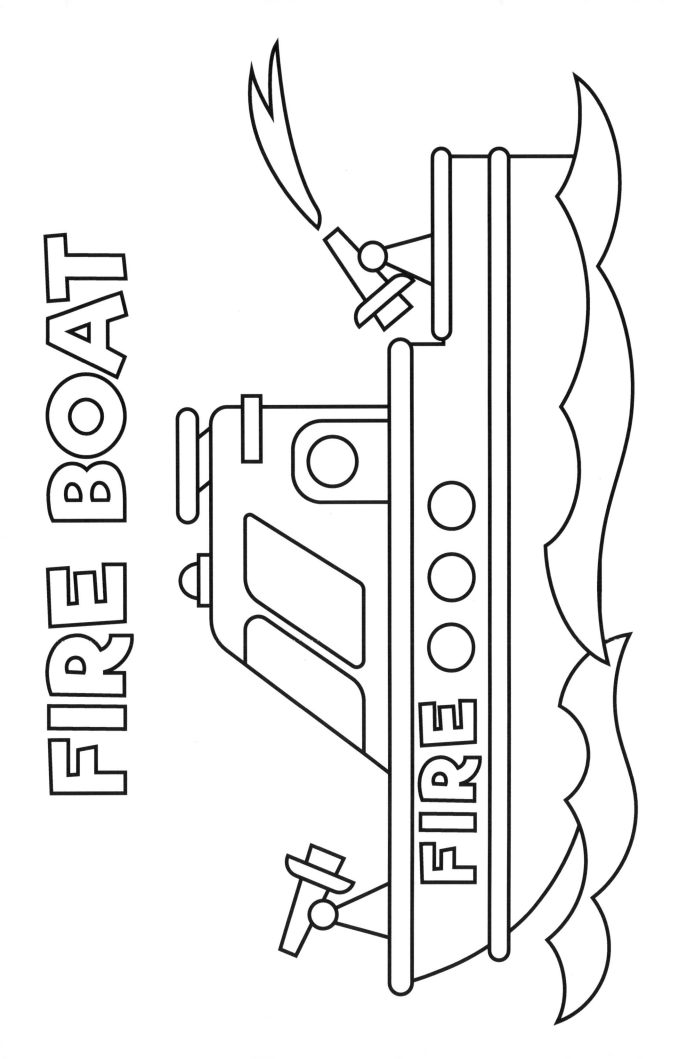

FIRE BOAT

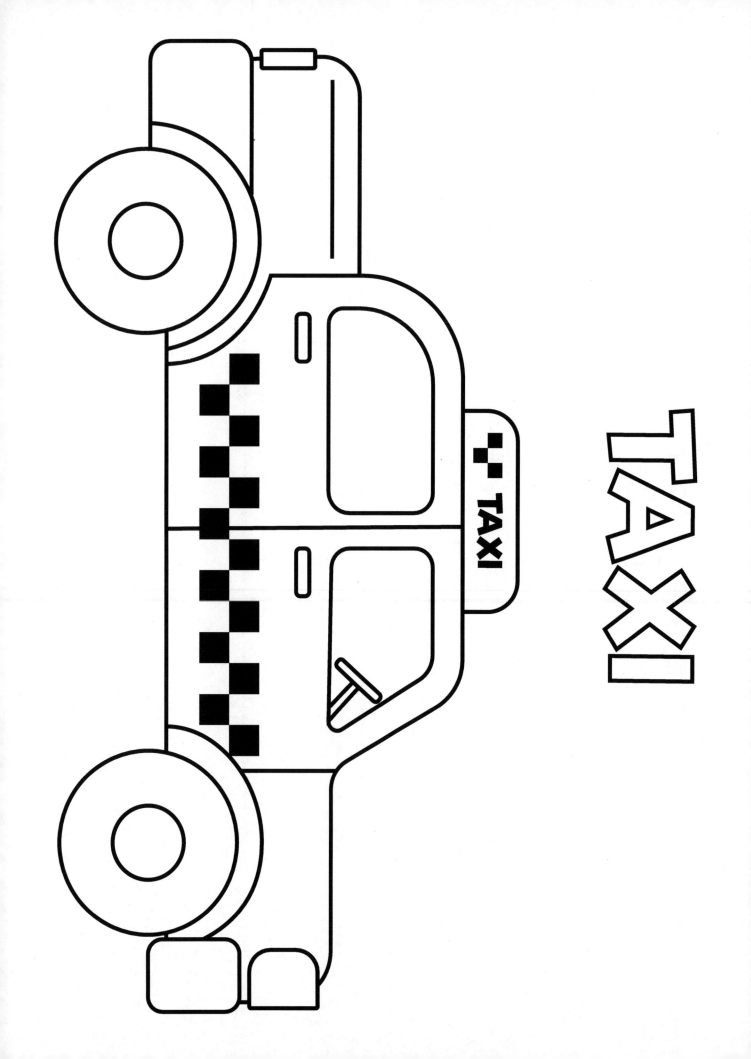

TRACTOR

SEAPLANE

PASSENGER PLANE

MINI EXCAVATOR

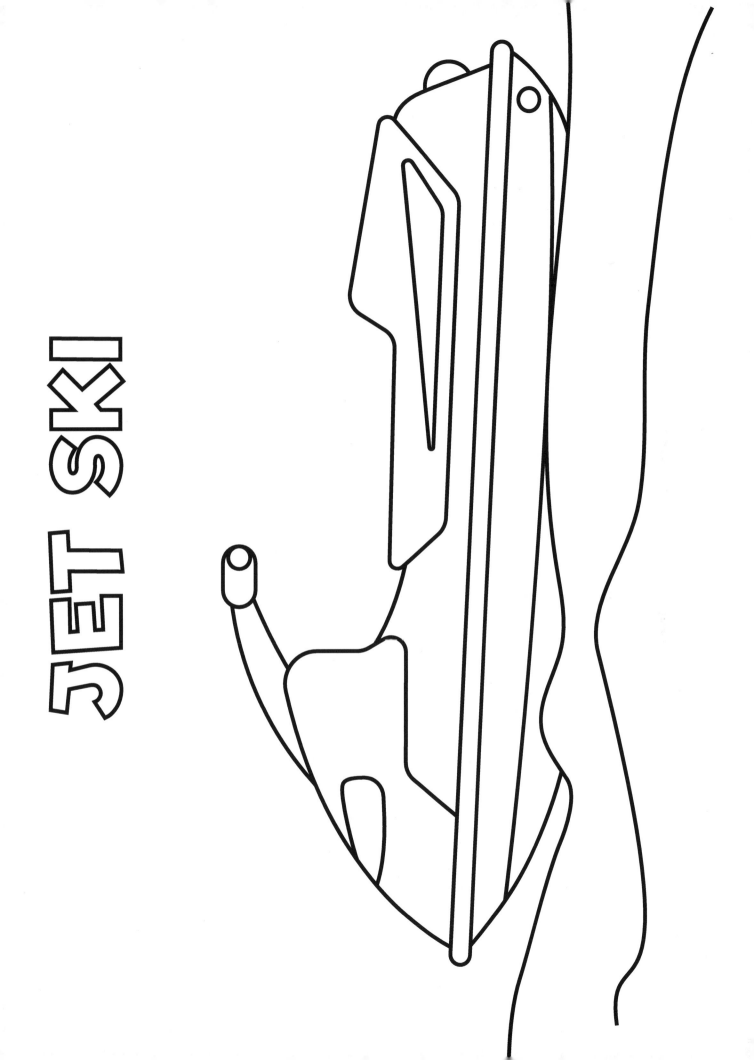

JET SKI

FRONT LOADER

FIRE ENGINE

UNICYCLE

TOW TRUCK

STAGECOACH

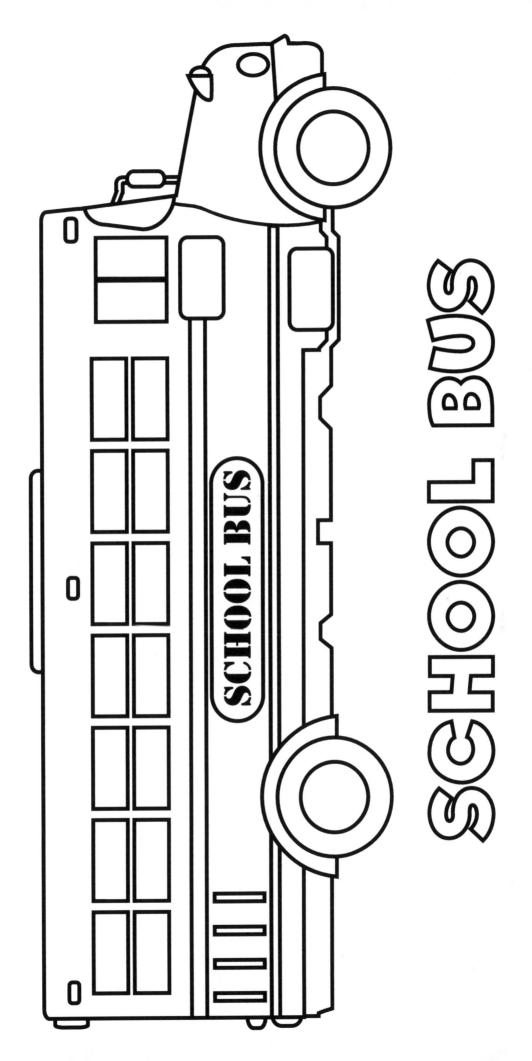

SCHOOL BUS

QUAD BIKE

FOOD
TRUCK

MOTORBIKE

DUNE
BUGGY

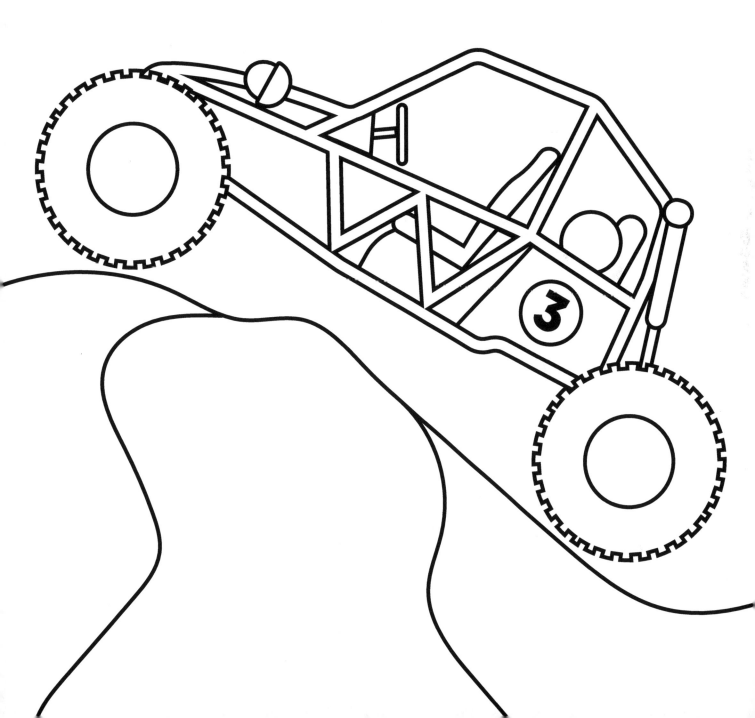

DOCK CRANE

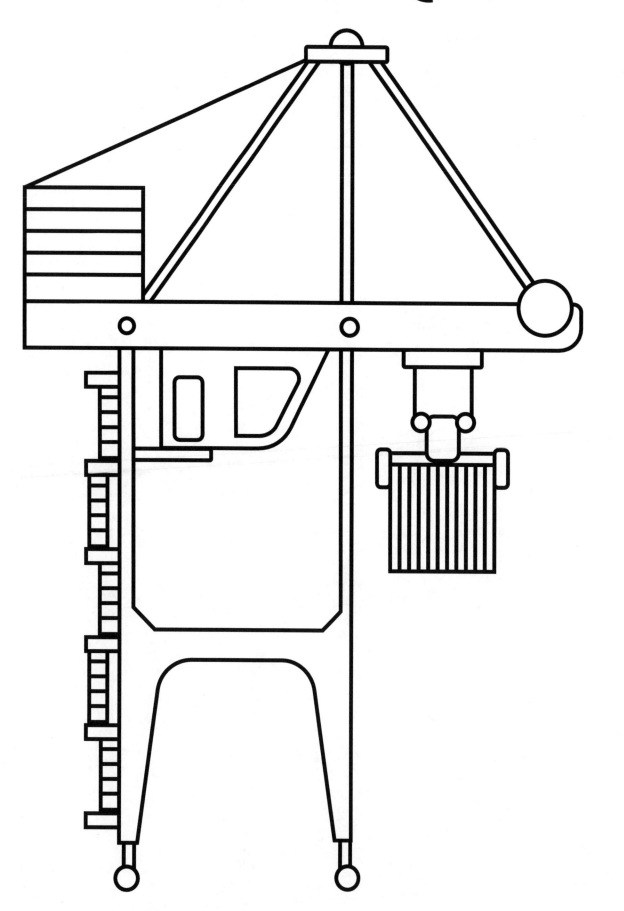

COMBINE HARVESTER

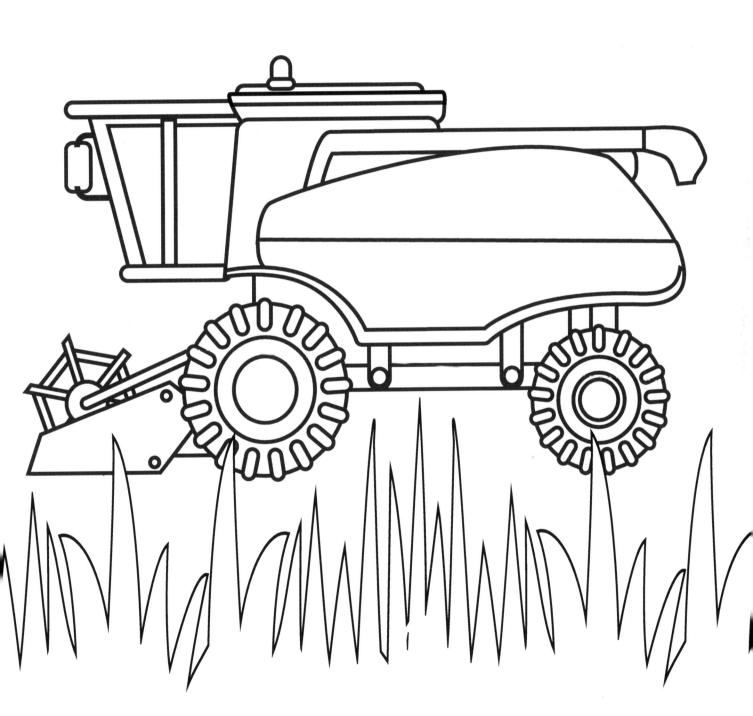

BIPLANE

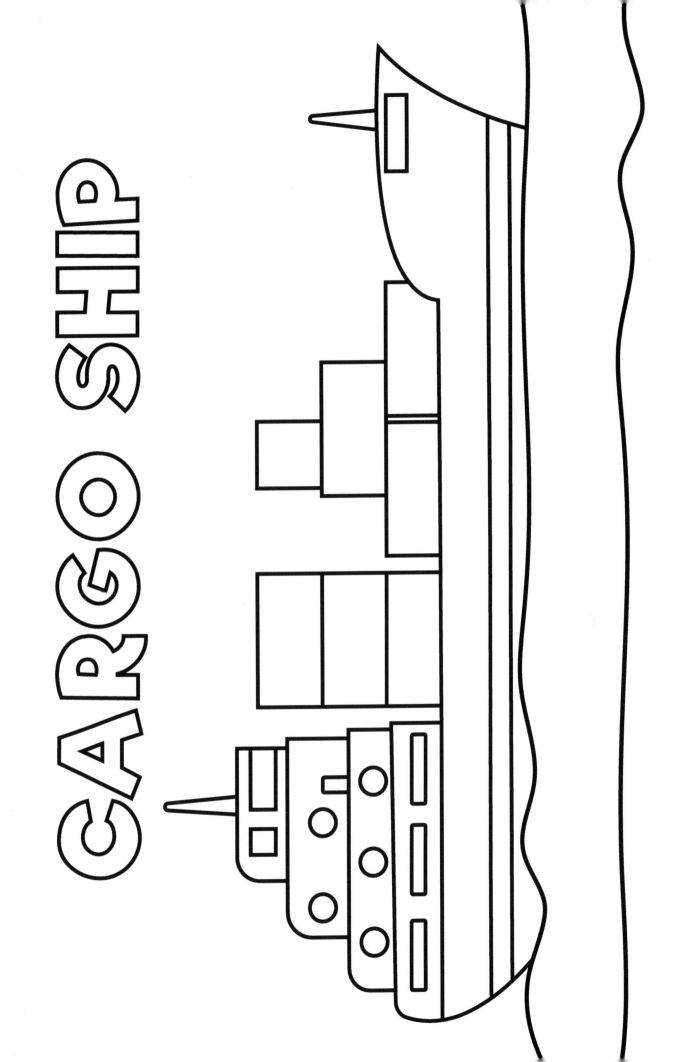

CARGO SHIP

AIRCRAFT DE-ICER

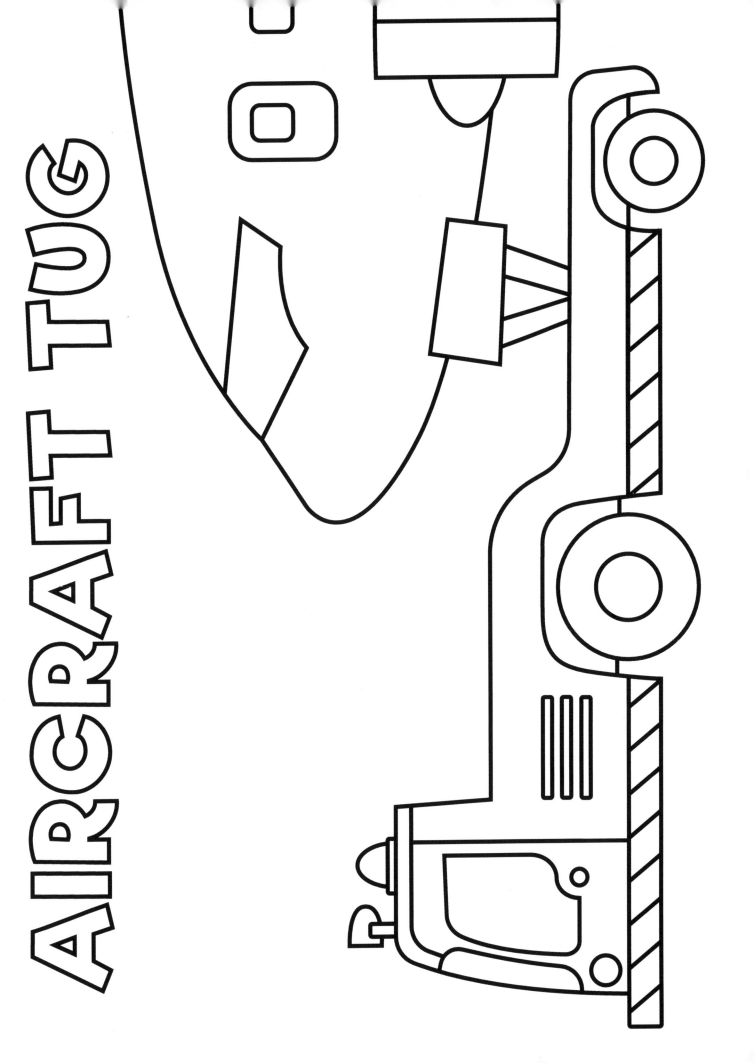

AIRCRAFT TUG

POLAR EXPLORER

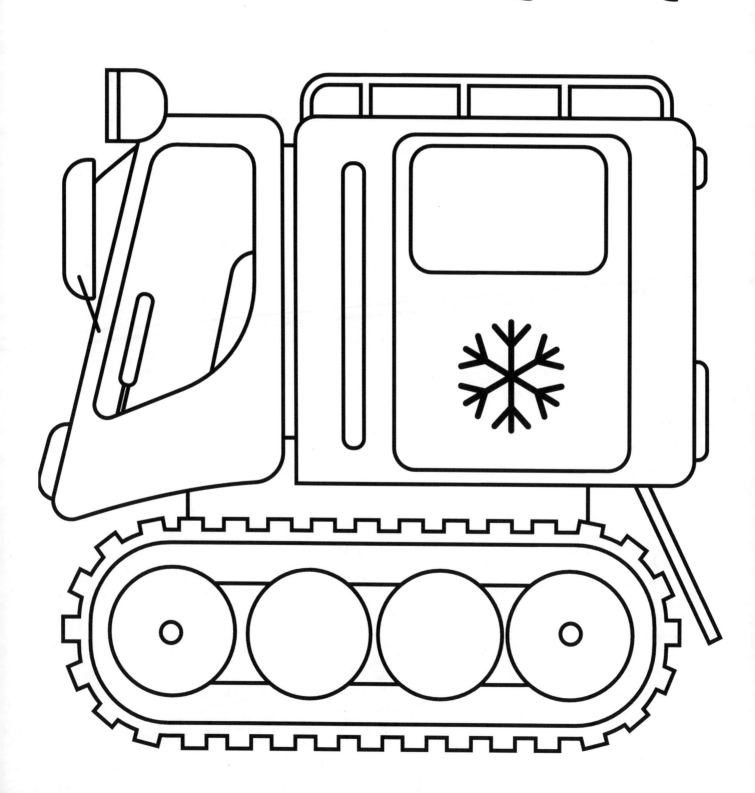

HELICOPTER

TANDEM ROTOR

FIREFIGHTING PLANE

RACING CAR

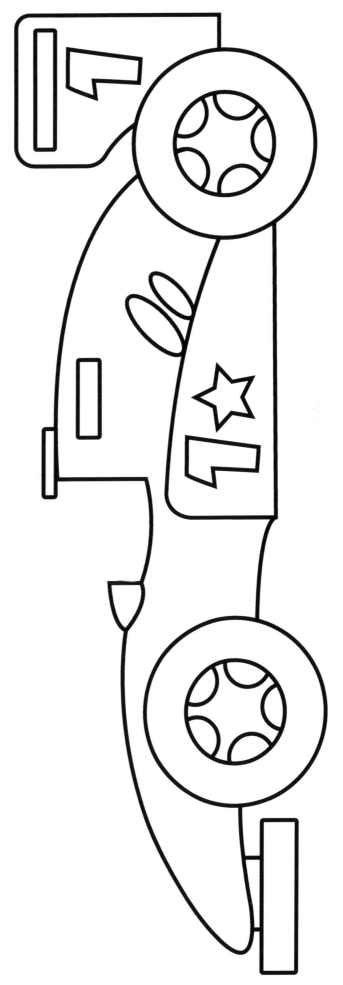

DRONE

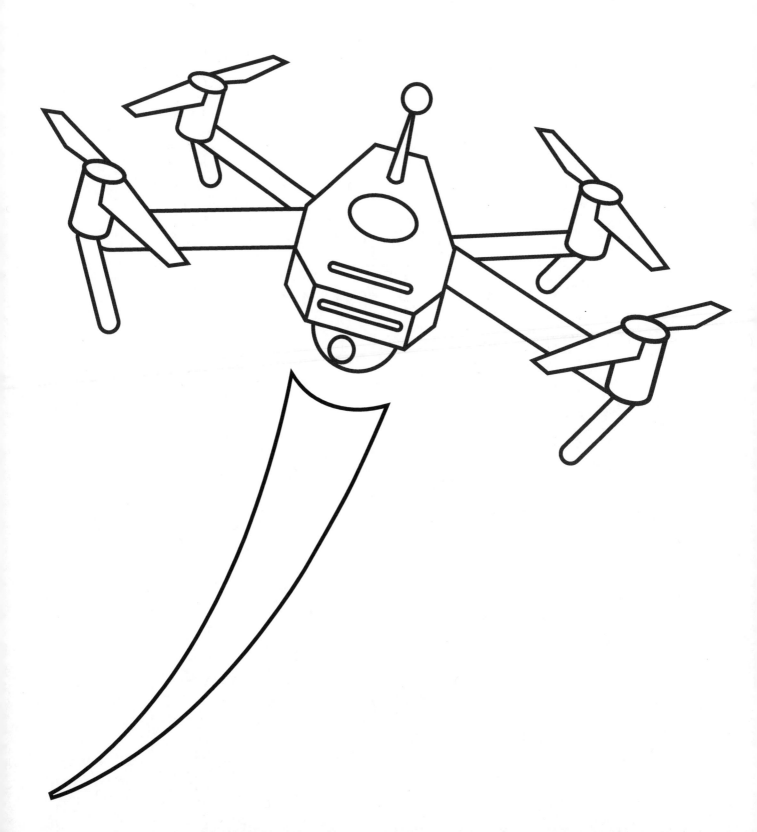

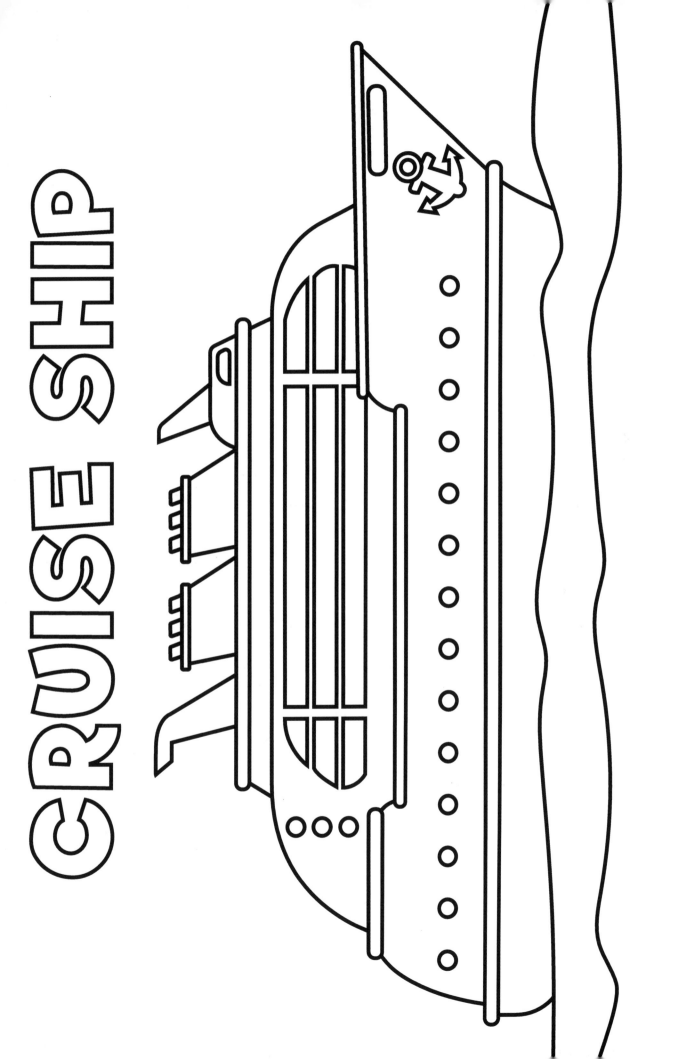

CRUISE SHIP

SNOWMOBILE

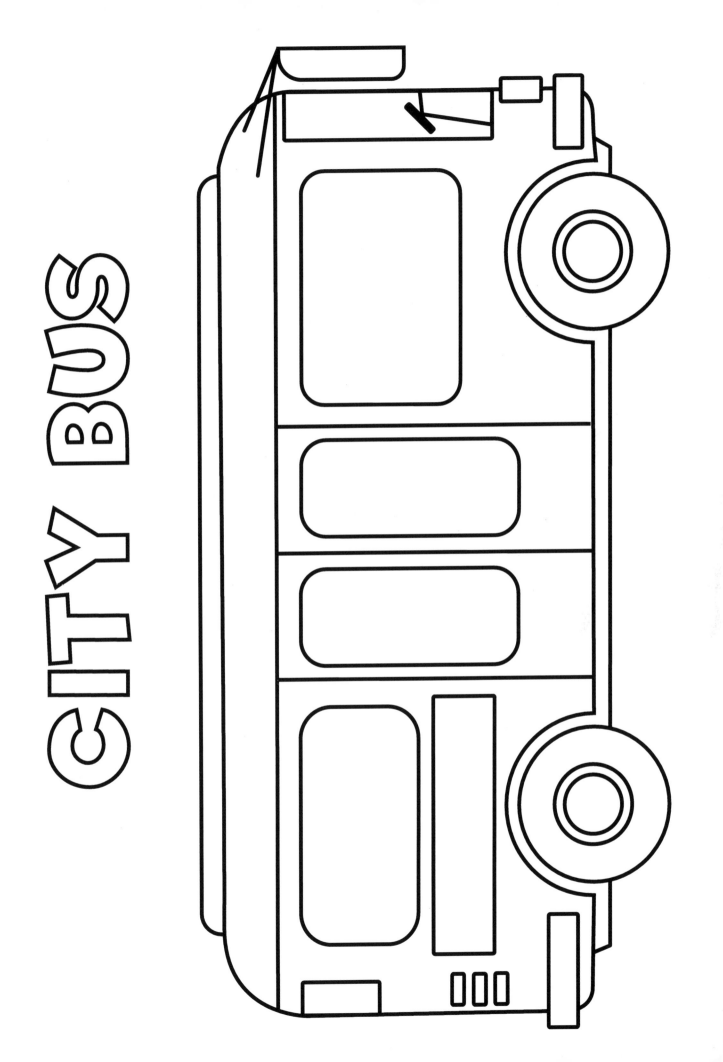

SLEIGH

RV MOTORHOME

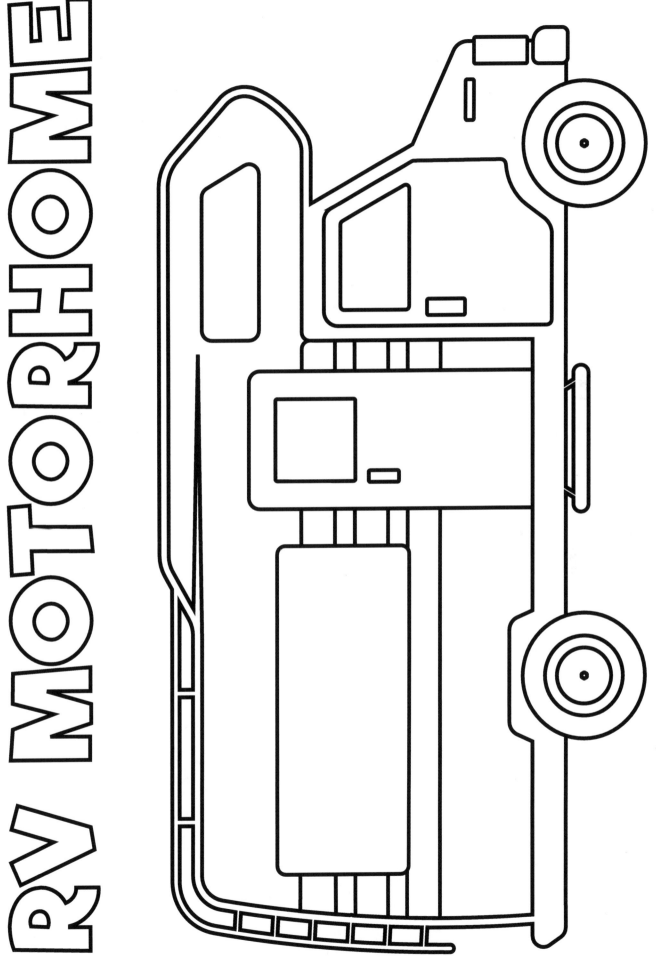

ROAD SWEEPER

PICKUP TRUCK

DEMOLITION CRANE

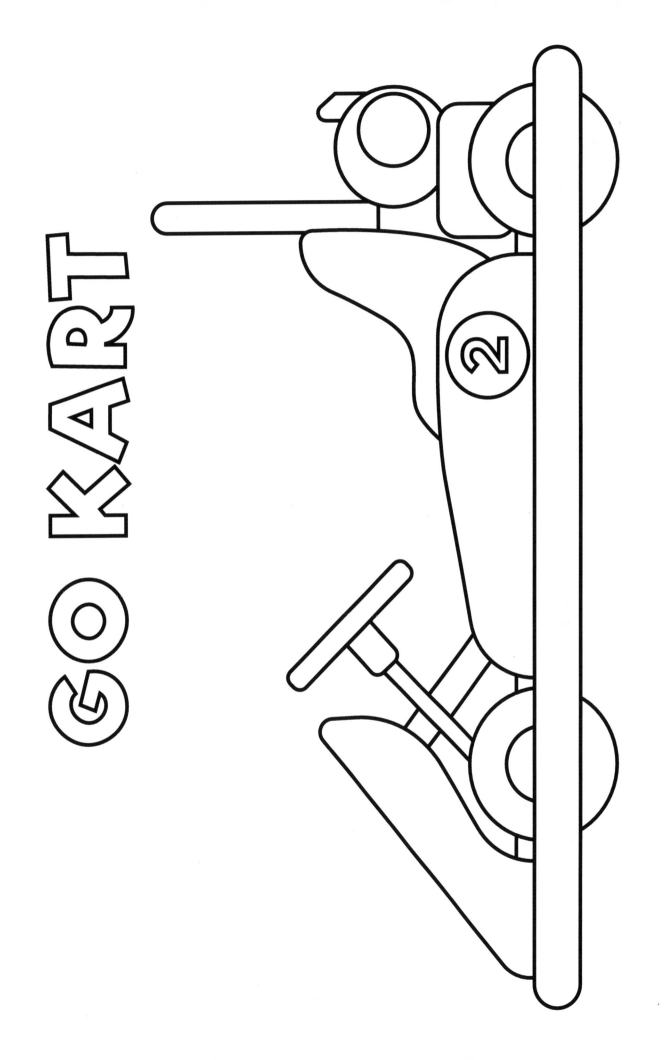

BLIMP

CARGO LOADER

AIRPORT

ARMORED TRUCK

AMBULANCE

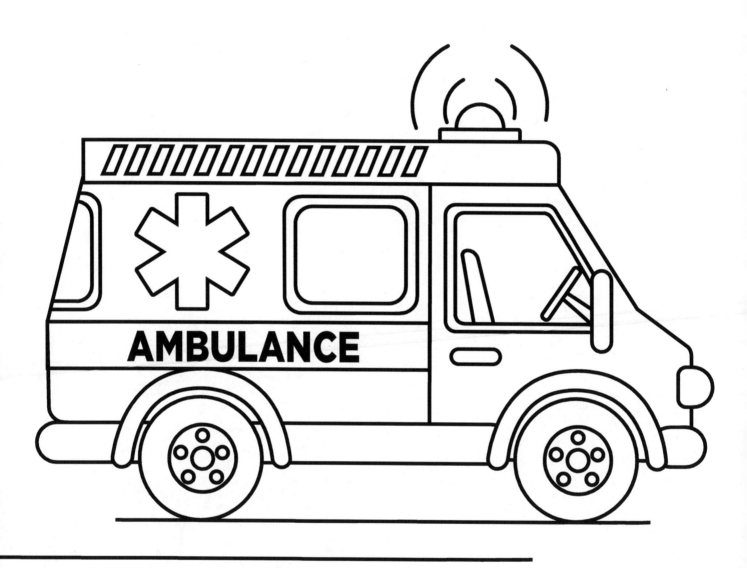

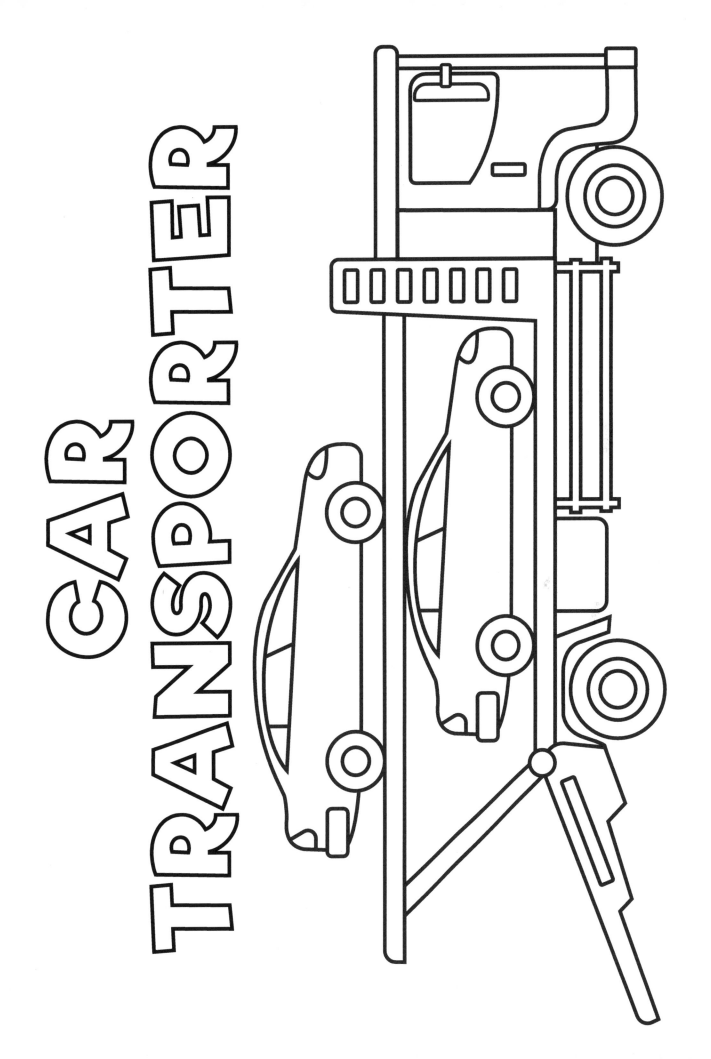

CAR TRANSPORTER

POLICE CAR

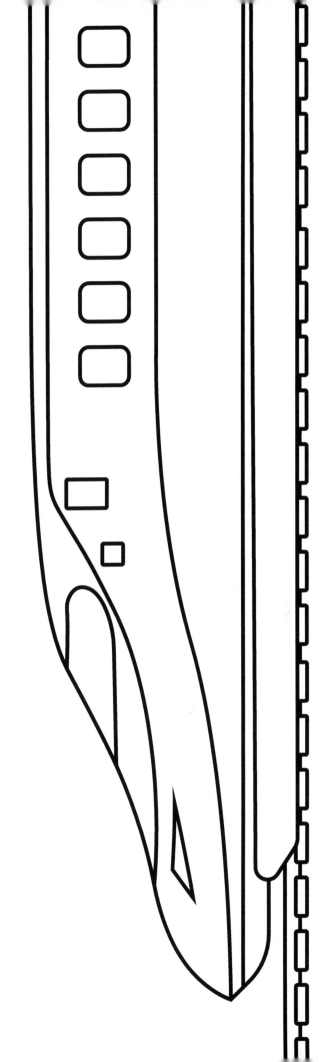

BULLET TRAIN

CHOPPER

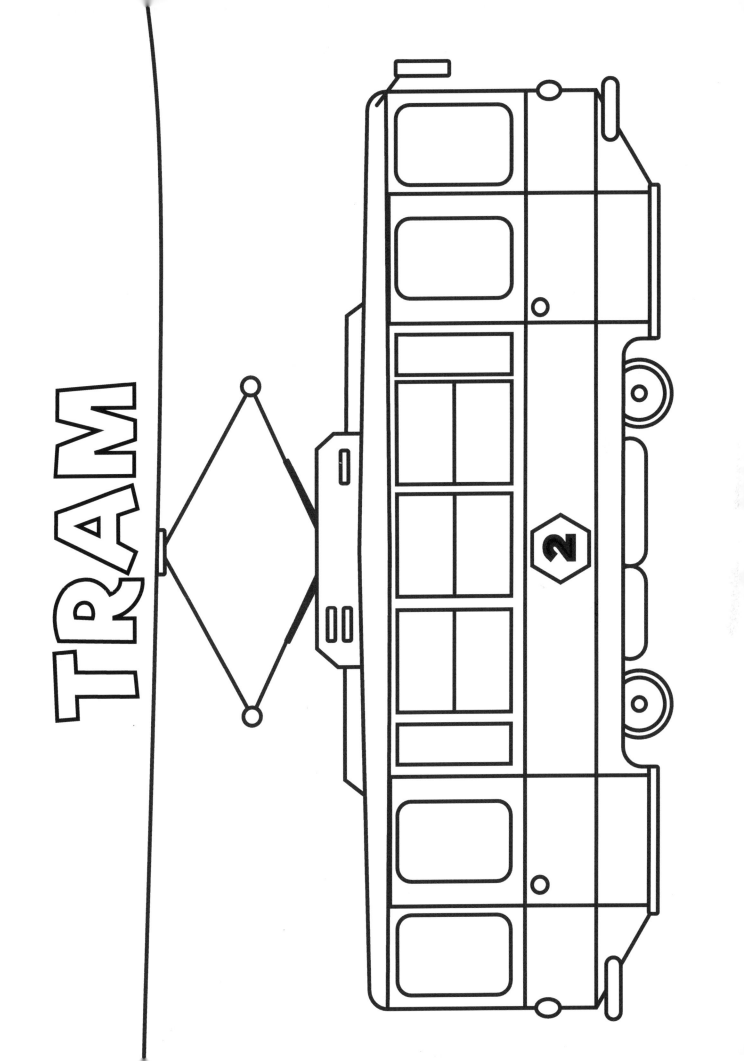

TRAM

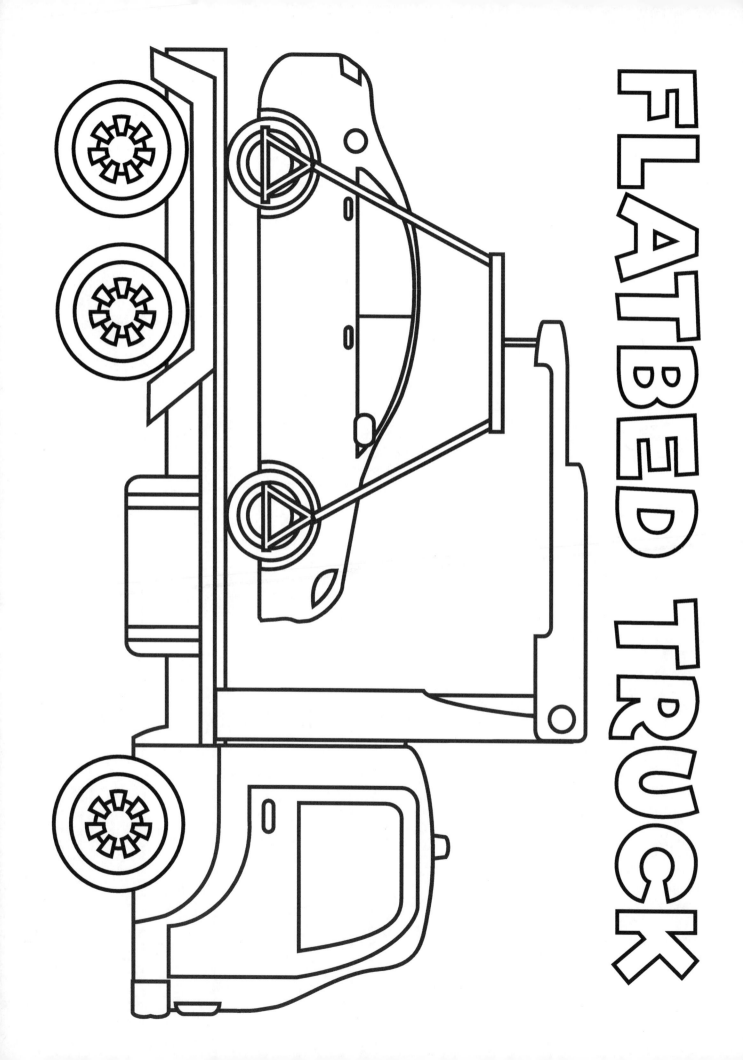

FLATBED TRUCK

FREIGHT TRAIN

We hope you enjoyed this book. As we learn and grow, we'd love a rating or review for it on Amazon, if you have time. **Thank You!**

Loads more from Under The Cover Press

available at amazon

ISBN 979-8864951200

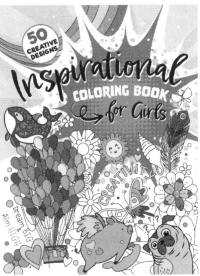

ISBN 979-8430304089

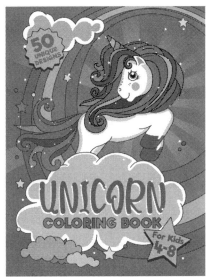

ISBN 979-8695161878

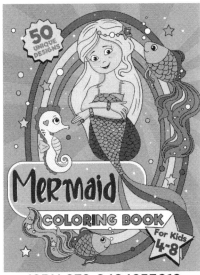

ISBN 979-8484253012

ISBN 979-8590346219

GROWN UPS!
VISIT US AT
UnderTheCoverPress.com

OR SCAN TO VISIT US

• FREE STUFF • NEWS •
• INFO •

ISBN 979-8559845876

ISBN 979-8559850436

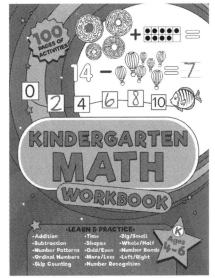

ISBN 979-8717778565

Made in United States
Orlando, FL
19 November 2024

54125290R00059